Dedicated to love...
love of my brother Ricky for his inspiration,
love of my uncle David
who taught me entrepreneurship on the family farm,
love of my father who introduced me
to the construction industry, love of my friend Dwight
for believing in me, love of my wife Deb,
son Barry A., daughter Stayce and family
who encouraged me to follow my dream
and love of the great Schlouch team,
customers and associates who make our company
the success it is today.

ROADMAP TO EXCELLENCE

**A guide to achieving success
and excellence in your work
and in your everyday life.**

BY BARRY L. SCHLOUCH

"The quality of a person's life is in direct proportion to their commitment to excellence, regardless of their chosen field of endeavor." Vince Lombardi

Introduction–Why am I writing this book?

The purpose of this book is to draw on my experience in construction to support our employees and the 8 million (and growing) workers in construction today. It is intended to help them achieve excellence in construction and to grow and prosper in their own lives. This book is also very helpful to anyone who wishes to pursue excellence in his/her life and contribute to not only his/her own personal growth but to approach his/her daily work as an opportunity to help and serve others.

In 2005 I read a trade magazine article that really made me think about the profound impact the construction industry has on the world and the huge opportunities that lie ahead for those of us in the business. I learned that there were over 7 million jobs in the U.S. construction industry which was 5% of all jobs in the U.S. Job growth was up 3.8% translating to 258,000 new jobs, double the 1.7% average US job growth for the year. The average wage was $19.34 per hour, 22% higher than the average of all private industry non-supervisory workers. The construction value put in place in the U.S. had exceeded 1 trillion dollars, which was then about 8% of the GDP (gross domestic product). Shipments of materials and supplies totaled $470 billion, which was 11% of total manufactured shipments. According to the Census Bureau, there were 710,000 construction establishments in 2002 of which 91% had fewer than 20 employees, 1% had 100 or more and the average number of employees per firm was nine people.

I find it so fulfilling to devote my life's work to the construction industry and I am excited about the future of our industry. What excites me is that every construction site we work on is different; each local town has its own rules, we have to deal with a variety of weather conditions every day, and the work we do improves peoples' lives. I feel like I'm on an "outward bound journey" every day! My talents in creativity, innovation, entrepreneurship and problem solving, backed by an incredible team, support me on this journey so that I can accomplish my goals.

Drawing on my personal success as a construction laborer to co-founding and building our company with my wife, Deb, I have discovered five key principles for success.

- Keep a "kindergarten state of mind" and learn everything that you can to continually improve yourself.

- Always give it your best, practice excellence in everything you do and get a little better everyday.

- Be willing to help others in any way that you can.

- Be open to new opportunities and step in to those opportunities with a "can do attitude".

- Open your eyes and heart to see the big picture and learn how everything works together to make every day a better day!

When I started in my first construction job as a laborer 30 years ago, it seemed like a maze at times to figure out what I had to do that day and what I needed to know to succeed in my role. What were the job site plan and goals for the day? Did we succeed in achieving the goals each day? What skills did I need to acquire to advance? How could I make a positive impact? To my knowledge, there was no guidebook then and I am not aware of one today. Our daughter, Stayce, joined our company recently and started as a laborer. She had many of the same questions that I had 30 years ago. It was Stayce and others in our company who inspired me to write this book. While this guidebook will answer many of your questions and provide you with a sound plan to succeed and prosper, my hope is that it inspires you to achieve excellence in everything you do!

Excellence
In Construction

Table of Contents

Why we do what we do

In 1983, my wife, Deb, and I along with our one-year-old daughter, Stayce, and four-year-old son, Barry A., launched our business using our tiny basement as our office. At that time, I thought we were in the business to perform excavating and utilities work. As many amazing years have passed, I discovered that we are really in the business of altering the environment to meet specific human needs.

I'll never forget when I gave a presentation to a group of college students in an entrepreneur class and was asked, "How do you get excited about the dirt business?" I love it when people ask me that question today. I asked the students if any of them drove to the college that day. Lots of hands went up. I answered that the dirt and construction industry made that possible by building the roads to provide the means for them to drive here. I asked if anyone took a shower that morning and again almost all the hands went up. I let them know that our industry made it possible for the fresh water to flow into the buildings to take showers, drink water, flush the toilet and provide the sites for the house they live in, the school environment we're enjoying today, our work environments, religious environments, cities, hotels, parks, golf courses, bike and walking paths, waterways such as Hoover Dam, Disney World and all sorts of entertainment. All this was made possible by the "dirt business" and our industry as a whole. At this point I'm jumping up and down with excitement and the room was completely quiet with all eyes locked on me. I sensed a paradigm shift just occurred. I was able to raise their awareness about why I get excited about the dirt business. The greater purpose truly is to improve peoples' lives worldwide!

I was blessed having the opportunity to grow up on a family farm, which was a very entrepreneurial experience. Many farmers appear to have little material wealth but are blessed because they possess a love for the land and great wealth in creativity, innovation and entrepreneurship. There is a genuine love for working outdoors in the environment. I knew then that my calling was to work with the earth and be outdoors. My farming background provided me with a solid foundation to build a great construction company. I never forgot how my uncle David took the time to mentor me each day on the farm and I realized at an early age the importance of helping others to learn and grow. I loved every moment and realized later that the greater purpose of farming is to feed the world. I had a part in that mission of improving peoples' lives!

Like farming, we do construction for the love of the land and to be connected to "Mother Earth", utilizing her resources to do what needs to be done. I am more excited today than ever about what we do! I know that when we build the next road for a housing development, people will soon have new houses for their families. When we prepare a new site for a shopping center, new jobs will be created and people will buy food and clothes to care for themselves and their families. When we prepare a site for a new manufacturing plant, warehouse or office, more jobs will be created and a means created to better service the needs of people. When we provide a site for a new school, it will provide a comfortable environment for people to learn. How can you not get excited about this?

Build YOU First!

I have learned from one of my mentors that attitude is a composite of your thoughts, feelings and actions. In order to benefit from this guide and achieve success in what you do, you must first have a "can do" attitude.

Your attitude breaks down into 3 parts, the conscious mind (thoughts), subconscious mind (feelings) and body (actions). The composite of these 3 parts is what will create the results in your life. I must admit that at times I have a negative attitude. However, it is short lived and can be changed at any moment with a simple decision to have a positive attitude and get back on track. Make your attitude a "CAN DO ATTITUDE!"

As a child on the farm, I learned everything I could about farming from anyone who would teach me. I had great teachers and mentors. By the time I was 16 years old I could perform any task on the farm. I understood the farming process from tilling the land to planting the seed, nurturing the growth and harvesting a beautiful crop.

Shaping your attitude is very similar to nature's law of harvest. It requires the seeds of good and worthy thoughts to enter your mind. The subconscious mind is like the fertile soil needed to receive your positive seeds of thought. Keep in mind that seeds do not grow on a rock. You must have an open, fertile mind to harvest bountiful results in your life.

I remember when I worked as a construction laborer at age 19, arriving every day with my can do attitude so that everyone wanted me on his/her crew! I learned about everything I could in construction and how to do it the right way. When working as a surveyor for a civil engineer at age 21, I would go from office to office on rainy days asking all the engineers how I could help them. After becoming skilled in surveying, I learned storm water calculations, earthwork cut/fill take off, and also excelled in blue print reading and project design. As a young surveyor, I wanted to become an instrument man. My supervisor told me that before he would let me become the instrument person on the crew, I had to set up the instrument in one minute or less. I took the theodolite instrument home on weekends and practiced setting it up on my own time. Within one month I was working on the crew as an instrument man! I believe that if you are going to work for someone or for yourself each day, you should give it your best and learn all you can! You've got everything to gain and nothing to lose.

I often refer to my attitude as a "kindergarten state of mind." Kindergarten was my favorite grade in school. My experience in kindergarten was simply amazing. We had time to learn, took breaks to play and rest each day. Don't forget the cookies and milk! I operated at peak performance every day, gaining a solid foundation for personal growth.

Make up your mind to work for the best company and be selective by picking one with competent people who are open to growing and sharing their knowledge. In construction, it is important to find out what you love to do most, learn from the best, do your job better than anyone else, learn about the big picture and share it with others. By investing in you and giving the best of yourself every day, you will bring good things to your life and to the people around you.

It is important to enjoy the work you do. My working process is like a state of professional play, incorporating that "kindergarten state of mind" and combining rest and rejuvenation in order to operate at peak performance. This process enables me to follow my plan and take actions each day toward achieving my goals. By doing this, I'm able to give the best of myself each day with an open mind to learning more. That in itself positions me for a better day the next day.

"There's always room for improvement- it's the biggest room in the house." Louise Leber

Understanding the big picture

To achieve excellence in construction, it is important to understand how the big picture works. Imagine playing a sport like football, stepping out on the field with your teammates and not knowing how the game works. It would certainly be chaotic and non-productive. The same goes for construction.

The construction process begins when a developer decides to build a project to meet a human need. Most of the time, the developer will follow the traditional way of building a project by hiring a separate architect and engineer to design it and then a contractor to build the project according to government code. This traditional process is called "design, bid and build." Each time a project is done this way, huge amounts of potential for improvements in design and construction are missed and these projects might run over budget and behind schedule. The quality of a project is a result of the quality of the project team.

Most projects take an average of two or more years to receive approvals from the various governmental agencies charged with regulating development. Therefore the time to brainstorm and incorporate the best practices in both design and construction to reach the most cost-effective approach is during the approval process. Unfortunately, most developers, designers and contractors miss this opportunity.

To create a better link between design and construction we added in-house design to our company to improve efficiency.

This story illustrates the inefficiencies of the traditional process: Several years ago we designed a shopping center that brought the best practices of both design and construction together. The cost estimate was $1.7 million to complete all the sitework. Just before ground breaking, the developer decided to sell the project to its two anchor retailers. I'll never forget when the retailers told me that they were unable to contract with us because corporate policy required an independent engineer to design the project and five contractors to bid it. They were following the traditional design, bid and build standard. The new owners proceeded to hire an engineer who took almost 2 years to design the project a second time. We were one of the five bidders and were awarded the project. We successfully built it on the same site for $2.4 million. The new project owners spent an additional $700,000 dollars and completed the project more than two years later! They experienced a 30% cost increase, lost two years of retail revenue, and because they didn't know any better, they were still happy. These types of lost opportunities occur every day in the U.S. construction market. The potential savings could be more $120 billion each year. Huge!

From my experience, the best approach to take is a "project team approach". The team consists of a competent developer, designer and contractor and has specific, clearly defined goals including a budget and schedule. The designer and contractor work closely with the owner in developing these goals through a feasibility study. Some important steps for the team to follow are working with an accurate topographical survey, identifying sub surface and soils conditions, balancing the earthwork, having an erosion control plan that works in synergy with both building the project and protecting the environment, placing utilities at the proper depth and location, using proper paving design based upon the soil conditions, and assessing potential safety hazards. A comprehensive project scope of work means there will be no hidden surprises later. This approach results in potential savings. This approach requires trust, integrity, competency and teamwork.

Most of our work today is still performed using the traditional design, bid, build approach and we are very successful working within this process. Unfortunately, by using this approach, opportunities are missed. These missed opportunities can result in added change orders, surprises and delays that usually result in an adversarial relationship between the developer, engineer and contractor.

At Schlouch Incorporated, we always practice a team approach. We deliver proactive solutions that result in on-time and on-budget projects. Delivering this product to our customers is what keeps them coming back. Today more than 60% of our business is repeat business.

"The achievement of your goal is assured the moment you commit yourself to it." Mack R. Douglas

Achieving the daily plan

Baling hay on our farm was a process that needed some improvement. The baler machine compressed hay into a 2-foot-wide by 3-foot-long bale weighing about 40 pounds. Sandwiched between a tractor and a wagon, the baler automaticaly threw the bales onto an enclosed wagon. Once the wagon was full, the hay is unloaded onto a conveyor and stacked in the barn and stored for animal feed. Usually filling five or six wagons in total, the same two people who loaded those wagons later unloaded them making for a long day. I discovered that if we had two extra people unloading the wagons, we could continue baling and double productivity.

Construction and the farming processes are very similar. The potential for improving efficiency is unlimited when you understand the whole picture, process, and plan. FMI Corporation refers to it as "Get Work, Do Work and Keep Score".

Get work!

A detailed estimate is presented to the customer that includes an itemized breakdown of each task such as the labor, equipment, materials and subcontractors. I like to say each project is built twice: first in theory in the estimator's mind, then in reality by the field crews. There can be hundreds of tasks like clearing, erosion control, earthwork, blasting, utilities, concrete and paving that are contained in the estimate. For example, let's say we need to move 10,000 cubic yards of earth on a site. The estimator has determined that two scrapers, two dozers, a roller, operators for each and a foreperson are needed to complete the task. If the estimator has determined that the crew can move 2,000 cubic yards per 8-hour day, then the crew could complete that job in five days. The estimate sets the goal for the team to meet or beat each day.

Do work!

Beginning each day with a morning huddle, the foreperson and team review the safety, quality, and production goals for the day. The foreperson "keeps score" throughout the day checking the team score card at lunch and day's end. Continuing with the example above, the foreperson discusses and tallies the scraper operators' daily production. Each scraper hauls 15 cubic yards per load. To move 2,000 cubic yards in one 8-hour day, two scrapers must load 134 loads, or 67 loads each. This is the goal and the tally of production lets the foreperson know if we are on target. This is the simple way to keep score and to keep the team informed.

Keep Score!

Have we achieved or beaten the production goals? Are we on target? If not, how do we get back on target?   These are some of the questions the foreperson might discuss with the team. A good support system for this process is important. Our company has always stressed the importance of good accounting to keep us on target. Opportunities to make changes are lost if production is not tracked daily. This is why the great companies tend to get the next great job!

Safety first!

The most important accomplishment of each day is for you to **go home safe and enjoy a wonderful dinner with your family.**

Safety starts with an awareness of the potential job site hazards, having the training to protect yourself and others, and consistent behaviors supporting a safe work environment EVERY DAY!

Imagine if you had no practical training or knowledge prior to the first time you drove a car. The result could be fatal for you or someone else. It's the same for entering and working on a construction site. Safety starts first with each one of us.

On a construction site, some potential hazards include safe trenching, confined space, materials handling and fall protection. OSHA, Occupational Safety and Health Administration, is a U. S. federal government agency designed to identify job site hazards and to train and protect workers from those hazards. The OSHA 10, a ten-hour course designed to teach you about the jobsite hazards and how to protect yourself, is a great place to start. This training provides the foundation to become a competent person.

OSHA defines competent person in 29 CFR 1926.32(f) as "one who is capable of identifying existing and predictable hazards in the surroundings or working conditions which are unsanitary, hazardous, or dangerous to employees, and who has authorization to take prompt corrective measures to eliminate them."

At the beginning of each day, the competent person leads the morning huddle and documents the discussion. This is where potential hazards and proper protection are identified. Here are some examples of what the competent person and job site crew monitor on the job site:

- Are the back up alarms on the heavy equipment working properly? These alarms alert everyone around that the machine is backing up.

- Are safe trenching procedures being followed? When a 5+ foot deep trench is being excavated, a complete trenching log and shoring system is necessary.

- Have all chains, cables and slings been inspected for safe operation?

- Is there a Confined Space Permit?

Do your homework and work for a company that follows this kind of safety format. Your life and the lives of others depend on it!

Safe working habits equal higher productivity. There is a myth that safety costs money. Yes, it does, however the initial investment in training and the use of safety protection equipment is paid back in improved productivity. Think of it this way, even if working safe did cost money, how much is your life worth? The bottom line is that when people are skilled and prepared, they are more productive. It's that simple.

Most important, having our teams working safe is the right thing to do!

The BEST do it RIGHT every time

Quality is a Schlouch Incorporated standard. I personally speak at our new hire orientations each month. I emphasize that the most important thing for new employees to remember is that when they go to our job sites our goal is to build each project right the first time, on time and within budget. To achieve this goal, our mission is to work safe, work hard, work together, work smart and improve ourselves each day.

As discussed in chapter 4, in the "get work" stage, each of the tasks in the estimate has a detailed procedure for proper completion. This is called quality assurance and must be done correctly. For example, when we are reshaping the earth on a site we might be cutting the soil on one side of the site and filling the other side. Earth lift thickness, moisture content, and roller weight combine to insure proper density. The proper compaction is determined through a soil analysis. When the soil is not properly compacted, the finished paving or the building itself could settle over time.

At Schlouch Incorporated, we use a team approach with the inspectors by including them in our procedures. The foreperson and crew understand the various quality assurances for any task that is being performed as well as proper inspection and documentation procedures. Many developers and government agencies employ independent quality assurance inspectors. We take the time to ask for feedback from the inspectors and have found that they become one of our biggest marketing resources for the next project.

Doing the work right also has a positive effect on our employees. We find that they are very proud to be associated with our company and that makes them more productive.

When we ask new customers and business associates in the communities that we serve what they know about our company, the answer is the same. "I always hear good things about your company." Doing a quality job is priceless!

"If one advances confidently in the direction of his dreams, and endeavors to live the life which he has imagined, he will meet with a success unexpected in common hours." Henry David Thoreau

Compensation and advancement

Our employees are the heart of our company and our wage and advancement program is designed with growth and success in mind.

When thinking about the course you want to pursue in the company, here are some key questions for you to answer:

- What do I want?

- Where is my passion?

- What job role fulfills my passion?

- What skills are required to do a good job and excel in that role?

- What skills do I currently have.

- How can I acquire the new skills?

- How can I contribute and advance?

Those answers will help you define your plan.

In our wage and advancement program, each job role is divided into 3 levels, entry, intermediate and advanced criteria with pay increases from level to level. Requirements and rewards are available for all employees to review. An employee's skills are assessed by forepersons and supervisors at employee evaluations for merit increases.

We closely track and monitor all promotions each year. Safety, quality, and production always improve when our individual and team skills improve.

Good communication and team building skills are essential for a foreperson and supervisor. Taking the time to give each team member performance feedback on an ongoing basis is crucial. Both also evaluate for merit increases and advancements. Through employee evaluations, they review the employee's goals, what they do well and how they can improve. Then they co-create a plan with the employee, do what is necessary to help the employee succeed with their goals and follow up.

During profitable years, a company-wide bonus is distributed. No one is left behind. This is our way of saying "thank you" to the entire team for making the year a success.

A company is only as good as its team. We do everything possible to support everyone to learn, grow and prosper. This is our future. This is how the best companies continue to increase productivity and provide great quality and service at a competitive price to their customers. This is what brings customers back and attracts new ones. We become one happy and productive family.

"The glue that holds all relationships together — including the relationship between the leader and the led is trust, and trust is based on integrity." Brian Tracy

Work ethic, policies and procedures

Our company has a well-defined company organizational structure that includes detailed employee and safety handbooks. This is very important to for each employee to know the answers to the following questions:

- Who is my supervisor?
- If I'm not treated fair by my supervisor, who do I talk to?
- What could get me fired?
- What is legal?
- What are the guidelines and procedures for me to follow to do my job successfully?

Although we work in a team environment at Schlouch Incorporated, it is important to know who makes the final decision and who has the authority to take action. The organizational structure clearly defines the responsibility, authority and accountability of the leadership and its relationship to employees. If you feel you have not been treated fairly, you will follow the chain of command. When you reach an impasse with your supervisor, set up a meeting with your supervisor to review your situation and then proceed to do so. Anytime you feel that you've been mistreated throughout the entire chain of command, you should not hesitate to talk to the president. In our company, employees are encouraged to voice their opinion.

The employee and safety handbooks include all guidelines that meet local, state, federal, Occupational Safety and Health Administration (OSHA) and Mining, Safety and Health Administration (MSHA) regulations. All new employees attend a detailed orientation on understanding the guidelines in our handbooks. Supervisors also receive continued training in the application of the handbooks.

It is important for all new employees to know: "What can get you fired?" This includes things like theft, no call/no show for work, repeated performance issues, and safety issues. Once employees have a clear understanding of what can get them fired, it takes away the fear of the unknown and they can be more creative and productive on their job. For supervisors, it is part of their job to treat all employees fairly and consistently according to our handbook. In addition, a competent human resource department assists all employees in practicing work behaviors that are consistent and in accordance with these guidelines.

Our employee and safety handbooks are always evolving as new local, state, and federal laws are passed. They also evolve as our company changes, through experience, learning and growth. While working within the law, we want our guidelines to promote trust, learning, personal and team growth, open communication, creativity, brainstorming and problem solving.

One of the fondest memories of my career occurred in 2000 when we were named the #1 Best Place to Work in PA. The award was created by former Pennsylvania Governor Tom Ridge to showcase Pennsylvania companies who treated their people well and encouraged them to grow and prosper. We elected to submit the required package detailing our work place philosophy and practices while 250 of our employees were requested to complete a 56-question survey for companies that employed over 250 people. At that time, we employed 290 people. We were alerted that we made the short list of the Top 50 Large Companies, but were still unaware of our placement. About a dozen Schlouch employees attended the event in Harrisburg where we were thrilled to receive the #1 Best Place to Work in PA! Deb and I just wept with joy!

"Do you realize if it weren't for Edison we'd be watching TV by candlelight?" Al Boliska

The right tools to do the job

In site construction, to achieve success, we need a skilled team to perform the work. However, to achieve excellence in safety, quality and production, that team MUST be supported with the right tools including items such as heavy construction equipment, trucks, vehicles, safety equipment and many other types of specialized tools. When the estimator prices the job, he or she combines all these elements to position us to be the safest, most productive, quality site contractor.

There are many questions and options to consider when the estimator as well as the foreperson and crew members select equipment and tools. It is important to match the operator with the best piece of equipment. For example, skilled operators are trained to safely operate and maintain their machines, combining knowledge of the most productive use of equipment within the specific task at hand. There are several ways to obtain this knowledge.

You can observe, take notes and learn all you can about the various tasks and processes. Change is constant. As technology changes, it is important to keep an open mind to new ideas and better ways of doing things.

Our company has changed from using blueprints, a 200-foot steel tape and a bundle of stakes to using Global Positioning System (GPS) technology to accomplish the goal with precise accuracy. The heavy equipment now has computers installed to communicate via satellite to provide instant, real time information to the operator, improving his or her grading accuracy.

A wealth of knowledge is available through the original equipment manufacturers (OEM) such as Caterpillar, John Deere, Volvo or Case and their dealer networks. When we started our company, we invited the experts from the various OEM's to evaluate our job sites and get their recommendations for the best piece of equipment or tool for the job. We use a team approach with OEM's and continuously build excellent relationships through trust and idea exchange and keep an open mind for new ideas.

When selecting a piece of heavy equipment, the goal is to have the lowest unit cost per task. This provides us with a competitive advantage when bidding the project. This is calculated by dividing the lowest owning and operating costs for the piece of equipment by the highest productivity. The OEM's can provide this information when evaluating a purchase.

At Schlouch Incorporated, our goal is to provide our team with the best technology possible. The average life cycle of a new piece of equipment is about seven years. When evaluating the best technology at SI, we involve our field and maintenance team, OEM's and our historical analysis to make the best decisions. The right fleet supports our team and our company to achieve Schlouch excellence in safety, quality, and production every day!

Training and rainy day opportunity

At Schlouch Incorporated, we know that skilled teams will be the most prepared to achieve excellence every day. We know that to maintain a highly skilled team we must invest in training. Each role in the company has specific requirements so training can be matched to the skills-advancement plan.

In addition to having a detailed job role, we have a clear and concise safety program, employee handbook and benefit program to use in training. The training process starts as soon as a person joins our team through a detailed orientation. This provides the foundation for team success. We also provide various training programs year round such as OSHA, MSHA, CPR/First Aid, Smith System Driver Training and a multitude of specialized training from our equipment manufacturers, trade organizations and schools.

The training begins with YOU. Find out what skills are required to master whatever role you perform. A self-assessment will help you design a training program with your supervisor to acquire those skills. Invest in YOU!

Once you have developed your plan you can find many places to learn. Company training programs are a great place to start. Your supervisor or co-worker can mentor you on the job. Books, DVD's, trade schools, colleges and online training are also available. Reach out and you will find it.

When I was 20 years old, I worked as a construction laborer with my dad on a project near Philadelphia and became interested in learning about surveying. I spoke to the lead surveyor about all of the skills required to become a competent surveyor. Part of my training plan included several college courses in math and surveying. I started my classes and continued through the winter to study surveying and soils and engineering while I was temporarily laid off from work because of adverse weather conditions. In between classes and studying, I worked part time on the family farm to help support my wife and son. The unemployment paychecks took care of our basic family needs and the extra money that I earned on the farm paid for my college tuition. When I was called back to work the next spring, I continued in night classes to complete the surveying program. Shortly thereafter, I had the skills necessary to land a full-time job in surveying. Little did I know that one day, these skills acquired during the rainy day and adverse weather periods would provide me with the essential skills to start a company.

In construction, adverse weather may be seen as negative because there is no work on the job site or pay for that particular time frame. However the positive is that you have the time to invest in yourself. Plan ahead and take advantage of rainy day opportunities! Most training today can be done on the computer. If you do not have a computer, ask your company if you can use one of their computers. I guarantee you that once you demonstrate to your company your willingness to learn and increase your skills, other opportunities will come your way.

"Individual commitment to a group effort. That's what makes a team work, a company work, a society work, a civilization work." Vince Lombardi

The ecosystem effect

Our success can only be possible through alignment with and support of our customers, vendors, associates and the communities where we work. We refer to it as a healthy ecosystem when we work in harmony with each other. As we see in nature when all is healthy, every aspect prospers.

We are very proactive in our support of a healthy ecosystem.

First, our customers are our employer. Without them, we have no jobs. We make sure we understand what they want in order to prepare ourselves to deliver it. We continually monitor the progress to make sure we are delivering what was contracted. Feedback is documented and shared with our team to continually provide our customers the excellence they deserve. We've also conducted full day customer think tanks to project their future needs and better position our company to meet them. Our desired customer experience is simple: deliver solutions that result in on-time, on-budget results to keep them coming back.

It is very important that we select the right customers who are in harmony with our company's values. We look for customers who are as innovative as we are, pay their invoices on a timely basis, support a safe work site, demand quality, and value long term relationships. These are the results: over 60% of our annual business is repeat business.

In addition to our talented employees, we value the support and expertise of our vendors and associates. We make sure that we select quality vendors and associates who respond to our needs by working safely, providing quality, efficiency and innovative ideas. Each year we host vendors' and associates' luncheons where we share the year's results and plans for the upcoming year. We also request feedback for ways to improve our company. They appreciate that we take the time to listen to their ideas. This is how we build the alignment, teamwork, and trust in our healthy ecosystem.

This healthy ecosystem also includes government employees, inspectors, and members of the communities where we work. All projects need numerous permits according to local, state and federal guidelines before any work can take place. We take the time to get to know them and include them in our processes. We have earned the reputation for doing a job the right way, therefore we are always welcomed back.

Last, but very important: the general public drives by our sites every day. Here's the picture that we want them to see:

- Each site has a beautiful job sign proudly displayed.
- The materials are placed in an organized fashion.
- The site is graded smoothly and sealed off each day with a roller.
- Our people are working in a safe and productive manner.
- There is no trash on the site because it is kept very clean.

Many of our new customers find us by passing one of our sites and say "Hey, I went by your site and really liked what I saw, I'd like you to do my next project."

Our healthy ecosystem results in a safe, quality, productive and prosperous environment for all!

" If your actions inspire others to dream more, learn more, do more and become more, you are a leader." John Quincy Adams

The leadership role

The responsibility to inspire and achieve excellence in construction starts with the leader of our company. I take 100% responsibility for my life, my feelings, my actions and all results that I get. I love Earl Nightingale's definition of success, "The progressive realization of a worthy ideal." I believe achieving "excellence" in any field of work is a worthy ideal.

I began to discover my leadership qualities at a young age. In junior and senior high school, I took a strong interest in becoming the best in the sport of wrestling. I gave my best at practice, conditioned my body through extensive fitness training, attended off season wrestling clinics and remained very focused on improving myself. What made it easy was that I loved wrestling. The results were very positive. I started on the varsity team every year. I was part of a county championship team. I was well respected for my talents and commitment but what came to me as a surprise as a senior was being unanimously voted the co-captain of one of the best teams in the county. I remember how I would strive for excellence and lead our team by example. About 15 years later, I received a lengthy letter from one of my former teammates who was going through some tough personal challenges in his life. In the letter he let me know how much I inspired him during those wrestling days and that it helped him get through his challenges at hand.

At Schlouch Incorporated, we have a comprehensive leadership handbook. Prior to becoming a leader at Schlouch, a person must understand the requirements outlined in our leadership handbook. The key sections include the role of the leader, the work place philosophy and practices, the vision and mission, a detailed history of the company, the business plan and model, company/ personal goals and detailed action plans. We also have a continuous training program to support our leaders as discussed in chapter ten.

I personally meet with all of our leaders at the beginning of each year to provide additional training on the leadership handbook. I also ask each leader to write up to five personal goals, five business goals and five suggested goals for the company and me. I devote the entire week meeting with groups of 20 and it is one of the most inspiring weeks of my year. I have found that when personal and company goals are in harmony there is no stopping us! The outcome of this process leads us to mutual understanding, focus, alignment and action.

As a leader, I am not threatened by the growth of our team, I am inspired. I take time every day to let our team know how much Debi and I appreciate what they do. We know it would not be possible to be the "#1 Best Place to Work in PA" and enjoy our quality reputation without them.

Whenever I meet with people about challenges, I do so with the intention to work things out and support the person or team towards reaching a positive solution. If it is clear that the situation cannot be resolved, I simply help him/her find another job where he/she can succeed. It just may not be at our company. It is not acceptable to keep a person employed at our company if he or she is not able to deliver. Keeping that person has a negative effect on our company and team. I'll be the first to admit that our company is not for everyone and that's ok. It is for the person who strives for excellence and is willing to improve each day.

It is important that each leader understands our company purpose, "Why are we here?", our vision, "What does it look like?", and our goal, "How do we achieve it?"

My mission statement is: "To live my potential to become the best that I can be."

It is your responsibility to be a great leader through your actions. Find out what you love to do, what you're good at and what customers value. When you align these three things in life, you'll hit what I call the "bull's eye to success". Live each moment giving your best and people around you will grow and feel inspired.

"The future belongs to those who believe in the beauty of their dreams." Eleanor Roosevelt

Anything is possible

Many people have asked me if I ever imagined when we started our company that one day we would employ hundreds of people and become a leader in the construction industry. I tell them I never realized it would grow to the size it is today, however I knew it would be great!

When I speak to college students today, I let them know about one of the most important decisions I've made in my life. It was the decision to ask Deb to be my wife and life partner. We met when I was 17 years old and we fell in love at first sight. We spoke one word that first night and that was "Hi". We were married in 1976 and she has brought only good to my life. The power of love can literally move mountains! It has and continues to do so for me.

Our company was founded with the ideal that "we can do things better". Shortly after starting our company, a friend gave me the book, "Think & Grow Rich" by Napoleon Hill. That book changed my life and woke me up to what was possible. I learned that it is important to find out what you really want in life. It has to be something that excites you so much that every cell in your body says yes to that idea! The idea evolves into a dream and then becomes a reality through goals and actions.

I am a dreamer. My third grade teacher once commented on my report card, "day dreams too much". It was true back then and it's true today. Dreams are important. Today we are living our dreams and I must say they are big! We will someday have a global company with a team of like-minded people dedicated to supporting our purpose in achieving excellence in a productive and prosperous environment that advances the quality of human life throughout the world. Anything is possible!

It is important for you to write down your answers to the questions in this book and determine your life plan. Gather a group of people in your life who support you and encourage you to pursue your goals. Give your life's plan the very best of you each day! I guarantee if you do this that you will eventually get what you want. Keep in mind that you may fall down many times along the way. I know I did, but I kept getting back up

25

with my "can do attitude".

It is my hope that by sharing my experience and the practices that have worked for me, some of these tools will help you to achieve excellence in your life.

" *If a person sweeps streets for a living, he should sweep them as Michelangelo painted, as Beethoven composed, as Shakespeare wrote.*" Martin Luther King, Jr.

Can you answer these important questions?

What are my dreams? Am I living my dreams?

What are the five key elements for success as defined in this book?

What skills do I need to acquire to advance?

How can I make a positive impact in the company?

What is the real purpose of site construction?

What is the impact of our work on the community?

What is the "law of the harvest" and how does it affect me?

Can you describe the meaning of a "kindergarten state of mind"?

What is the traditional process called for developing a building project?

Is there a better way than the traditional process and why?

What is a "can do attitude"? How can I improve my attitude?

How do we set goals for production and how do we measure them?

What is the most important thing I can accomplish each day on the job?

What is important to our customers?

What is an OSHA competent person?

What does an OSHA competent person look for on a job site?

What are the key questions I should answer in planning my role?

What are the key things a foreperson must consider in his or her role?

If I am not treated fairly on the job, whom can I talk to?

What is the daily goal for safety? Quality? Productivity?

What are my personal goals? Job related goals?

What could get me fired?

What are the things I can do personally to learn and grow in the business?

What are the ways I can get training to advance?

What makes up the Schlouch Incorporated ecosystem?

What should people see when they pass one of our job sites?

If I want to be a leader at SI, what must I know?

What is my rainy day plan?

How do you determine which is the right piece of equipment for the job?

What is important to the inspectors?

NOTES

About The Author

Barry L. Schlouch is cofounder and president of Schlouch Incorporated (SI). Starting from the basement of his small home in 1983, he has built an industry-leading site construction company serving Eastern Pennsylvania and surrounding states. Barry is a visionary and entrepreneur with the ability to bring his visions into reality. Through his leadership, Schlouch Incorporated achieved the status of being number one among large companies in the Best Places To Work In PA program in 2000. Among his objectives is to foster a culture where people are treated well and that encourages and supports creativity, provides solutions and growth of the individual and team in a safe work environment.

Before founding SI, Barry was vice-president of Rubright Construction, Inc. in Shoemakersville, Pennsylvania. Earlier he held survey and crew positions with Robert Ludgate & Associates of Reading, J. E. Breneman Contracting Engineers of Philadelphia.

A member of the Young Presidents Organization, Barry has participated for eleven years in the Executive Education Program designed for that group by Harvard University and has achieved alumni status. He also attended Penn State University and Lehigh County Community College and completed a two-year Executive Leadership Program at the Wharton Business School. He is a Certified Equipment Manager (CEM).

Barry and Deb Schlouch have two children, Barry A. and Stayce, both of whom are actively involved in the company. When not working or fulfilling one of the many speaking engagements he has during the year, he enjoys hiking, sailing, scuba diving and riding his Harley. In addition, he makes time for exercise, surfing, swimming, biking and personal growth.

Made in the USA
Monee, IL
16 December 2020